SMALL BOY BIG PROFITS
How Resilience and Mindset Can Change Your Life

BY

GARNET JR CHAMBERS

Small Boy Big Profits

Legal and Copyright Notice

The ideas expressed in this book are protected by copyright laws. Reproduction and distribution of any of the contents, in any form, without written permission from the author or publisher is prohibited, except in limited amounts approved by the copyright and fair use guidelines.

The author, editors, and publishers also fully disclaim any damages or loss incurred resulting from information provided or suggestions made in this book.

© GJR Publishing

Table of Contents

Acknowledgment	5
Introduction	6

Chapter 1: Building The Mind & Heart of an Entrepreneur 9

Game Rental King
Power of Frugality
Getting What You Speak!
Imagine Yourself!
Fake it Until You Make It!
Faith or Fear?

Chapter 2: The People in Your Corner 26

Mother of the Century
They Say No! So What?
Know Your Circle
"Locked Up"

Chapter 3: Stack Your Businesses Before Your Cash 41

Good Friends Are Better Than Pocket Money
Think Big!
Mentorship
Betrayal
Time Management
The Ultimate Power: Focus

Chapter 4: The Third Time's a Charm 65

Survival Mode

Chapter 5: You Are the Answer 73

You are the answer!

Chapter 6: Getting Out of Debt 75

Changing Your Buying Habits
Why Do You Want Money Right Now?

Chapter 7: Income Streams 80

E-Commerce
Real Estate
Email Marketing
Affiliate Marketing
Crypto Currency
Social Media Platforms

FINAL THOUGHTS 97

ACKNOWLEDGMENT

All praise to God! I have to thank our Heavenly Father for his protection and guidance. Nothing would have been possible if it wasn't for His amazing grace and power.

Special thanks to my parents, Novelette E. James-Chambers, and Garnett D. Chambers, for bringing me into this beautiful world. They have always been the primary source of inspiration for my entrepreneurial pursuits, energy, and work ethics. They showed me what it takes to be successful and that hard work is a must.

I would also like to thank all my friends and family members who pushed and encouraged me not to give up, especially during the tough times when I did not see a way out - special thanks to everyone! Sincere appreciation goes out to Shellon Samuels-White (editor), Donald Gadson Jr (voiceover), and writing coach for their encouraging words which gave me the strength I needed to face my fears as a writer. You all taught me to believe in myself. Writing was not something I saw myself doing, but because of your dedication to my success, I was able to complete this book. My success symbolizes determination, and resilience. I now believe that anything one envisions in life, can become a reality. Thank you all!

INTRODUCTION

I have always had a vision of becoming someone great. I wanted, like most persons, a lot of money, a lavish lifestyle, and to do whatever I wanted. I was determined, to be a very successful individual. Back then, I thought that having THINGS was what would make me a success. I now know that's not true success. I now see success, as working hard to accomplish one's goals, adding value to one's life, and the lives of others. Success will change a person's life. It is attractive, and people like to see it. They seek it, and even try replicate it in their own lives.

Small Boy Big Profits is not a book about getting rich quickly, rather, it underscores the idea that true success takes hard work and dedication. The contents of this book will show you that if I was able to overcome obstacles and misfortunes, you too can overcome and be successful in your endeavors. If success comes too fast, it will leave fast as well. Also, if you believe that life is too complicated, and there is no hope for you, I urge you to reconsider!

The key is to unlock your mind power, and change your mindset. It is important to acquire more knowledge: read inspirational books, listen to motivational content, learn from the past experiences of others, and most importantly, take action! My primary goal is to motivate, and show you that once you believe in yourself, and develop the right mindset, success is inevitable. This book is organized in three main sections:

The first section discusses the concept of *'mindset'*. Not everyone possesses a growth mindset. However, you can develop it. I have been fortunate to have made a lot of money, and have had numerous accolades at a young age: representing my graduating class as valedictorian, winning debating competitions, collecting awards and certificates for high achievement in different subject areas, and the list goes on. Unfortunately, I realized that I lost focus overtime. Fortunately, my tenacious attitude helped me to refocus and get back on track. There were periods in my life where it felt like a rollercoaster – sometimes high, sometimes low. I always wondered why this continued to happen. I later learned that my mindset, and my habits were not aligned, causing an imbalance in the success equilibrium. In this book, I will be examining some of these mindset habits that enabled me to change my life in a very positive way. You can learn from my experiences and carry them out in your own life.

The second section of the book is about **reducing debt**. There is good debt and bad debt. We all know that being in bad debt is stressful! Why don't they teach us about debt in schools? If they did, society would be far better. Money mismanagement results in bad debt and other negative effects! Most people don't want to have any form of debt, but most of the time, it's unavoidable. In this section, I will illustrate how I used good debt to clear my bad debts, and avoid debt altogether.

Finally, in the last section of this book, I will show you how you can acquire wealth to live the life of your dreams. I believe one should be independent and live life on his or her terms. Note: If you have a job or boss, please demonstrate good work ethics, as the by-product might be immensely lucrative.

Chapter 1:
Building The Mind & Heart of an Entrepreneur

No one can achieve success without the right mindset.

On April 6, 1995, I was born to two humble, hardworking, loving people: Novelette and Garnet Chambers. My name is Garnet Jr, a young, vibrant, tenacious lad. Both of my parents worked as room attendants. I was humbly raised in a small community called Sheffield, which is located about a mile from the popular tourist attraction Negril, Jamaica, a small island in the Caribbean. As a child, my parents were very hard working. Our home wasn't lavish. Instead, it was relatively small, peaceful, and tidy. This made it very comfortable. Everything we needed was provided. Seeing how hard my parents worked, influenced me to have a go-getter mindset, where I would continuously pursue to earn, live, and spend the way I wanted to.

My father played the role of disciplinarian. My mother was more calm-spirited and focused on acquiring knowledge through education. I continuously heard, "Knowledge is power" and "that's why I am sending you to school. The combination of their influence is what shaped me into the entrepreneurial-minded person I am today. My father's no-nonsense approach ensured I was always in line, and was on the correct path. My mother's persistence in becoming more educated greatly influenced my academic achievements through school. Although I was grateful for school, there was one thing that wasn't emphasized: financial literacy. I believe that a lack of this knowledge is why many in our society does not have the financial freedom we all want so badly.

My career as an entrepreneur was like a roller coaster where I had both some terrific wins, and some terrible losses. The fluctuation of wins and losses left me wondering why I experienced significant instability. I knew that it wouldn't always be easy, and I had to prepare for the hard times. It was overbearing at times. So, to realize my dreams, I sought to find a solution to the problems in my life. At the start of my entrepreneurial journey, my focus was making a lot of money!

I wanted to have a huge bank account, and run lucrative businesses. I strived to acquire this because the more money I had, the closer I would be to having a lifestyle similar to those I regularly saw on television. I moved forward to do just that, but along the way, I was facing a lot of trials, setbacks, and quite frankly, failure after failure. I just could not fathom what I was doing wrong. I started researching and reading self-help books.

The world of self-development taught me how to handle money, the mindset I should have, and the habits I have to inculcate in order to keep the money, and add value to people's lives. Positive thinking needs to be present to be successful. Being a positive thinker will position you to be confident, resilient, motivated, ambitious, disciplined, educated, tenacious, and passionate. I'd also say you should have the vision, troubleshooting skills, and most importantly, the willpower to overcome, not give up, and learn from the experiences of others.

Some of the people who have shown what real success is, are: Sir Richard Branson, Oprah Winfrey, Robert Kiyosaki, Albert Einstein, Curtis "50 Cent Jackson, Usain Bolt, Jeff Bezos, Elon Musk, Warren Buffet, Dale Carnegie, and the list goes on. These people have shown us their journey to success, which was not typical. Through willpower, tenacity, and resilience, they accomplished their goals. They had to work very hard, and went the extra mile in doing the things other people were not willing to do. Their experiences can teach us how success is achieved.

There are vital components that create massive success:

The people you listen to: you have to take or get advice from people who are in a place where you want to be, or who have the information you need. They can show you the direct path you should take to speed up your success. You don't have to 'wing' it all by yourself. You have to associate with people in the different areas of life you want to succeed in. Remember, success produces success.

Teachability index: This highlights how willing you are to learn and change. Often, most people are eager to learn about the tactic, strategies, and ways to enhance their lives successfully. However, when the time comes to take action and make the necessary changes, they are unwilling to do this. Being able to be coached into making right decisions is crucial.

The Training Balance Scale: Ninety percent (90%) of your thinking capacity needs to be successfully aligned with your goal, while the remaining 10% percent is executing the action. There is no way you can carry out a high level of work with a small thinking capacity. The growth of your mind is essential. Thinking the right way, and acquiring more knowledge (whether by reading, listening, or associating with like-minded people), will tremendously enhance how you feel. When Dale Carnegie (The World's Richest Man That Ever Lived at that time), instructed Napoleon Hill to study all the wealthy, successful men in the world, he wanted to discover the common denominator among them. From his research, he concluded that most men acquired wealth in many ways; he observed that their mindset, and high-level thinking were some commonalities in their success.

Before we get into the tactics and "things to do" that will help you experience massive success, Let's go back in time, to the beginning of my journey on the road to BIG PROFITS!

Game Rental King

It was April 6, 2004, when two of my mom's American friends - June and Eric, gave me my first computer - a Dell desktop PC, and a Nintendo Game Boy Advance (the clear bluish colored one). I was so happy to get these gifts that I just ran and hugged them; hysterically thanking them. I was the most satisfied ten-year-old child on earth that day! I brought the Game Boy everywhere with me: home, the playground, church, and even school, when I got the chance. I would typically play with my game boy at school during the two grace periods: break time and lunchtime. My world was complete! All was well until my classmates started watching my every step because they saw how happy I was. They wanted in on the fun.

I wasn't a selfish child, so I lent my Game Boy to my classmates so they could feel the excitement I felt every break and lunchtime. This continued for about two months, and it reached a point where all the boys in my class started playing, and this reduced my playtime. It became annoying, but I didn't want to be rude or seem selfish. I knew many of my classmates enjoyed the game, and it would be difficult for them to get one themselves. I did not know what to do!

One day, despite the turmoil and stress, a thought came to my mind. "Instead of lending the game boy for free, why not charge a small fee for game time?", I thought. So, I started renting my Game Boy for $50 per 15 minutes. This money I used to purchase more goodies at break time. This was the first business I started, representing the beginning of my entrepreneurial career!

At the time, I was making a pretty good amount of money, given my circumstances. In addition to this, my mother would typically give me an allowance of $150.00 JMD. Thus, the total income I would make from the game rental business allowed me to bring home $300 JMD every day. This was a 100% mark-up profit, excluding the money I spent on my lunch and break time.

Not only were my classmates enjoying themselves, but now I could enjoy myself as well. The earnings would allow me not only to buy toys, food, but other games as well. It was only natural that I expanded the business to maximize profits. This I did! Things were going tremendously well until I had arrived late for school one morning. As I rushed to attend a devotional exercise, I placed my Game Boy in my backpack and left it in my classroom. This was the biggest mistake I could have ever made! I did not know I was being watched!

As soon as the devotional exercise ended, and I returned to my classroom, checked my backpack for my game, and to my surprise, it was gone. I was, flabbergasted, anxious, and furious all at the same time. I looked everywhere, but it could not be found. I could not concentrate for the entire session. Someone had stolen my game boy! I just knew someone had to have seen something! So, I investigated, to no avail. There was no luck figuring out who stole my game, and no one came forward with any information that could help me.

How could someone steal my money-making machine? I was so disappointed, but what hurt the most was telling my parents what happened. I had not mentioned to them that I had my own little business. I was so caught up in making money, and enjoying life as the school king!

There was something else to note. This was my first failure at business. I did not see this coming at all, and as a result, not only was I affected mentally, but I quit the game business and gave up playing games altogether. I never played a game again until 2010, when I joined the chess club in high school. My entrepreneurial dream in the gaming world had been shattered, and that pursuit dampened like water on fire. Nonetheless, one good thing came from that experience, it allowed me to look for business ventures in different places. The taste of entrepreneurship was so sweet!

As an entrepreneur, there will always be a point in your career when tragedy strikes. You might lose your capital, the entire business, friends, and even members of your family. Periods like these are just a part of the process. The goal is never to give up. Learn how to be resilient and confident in hard times. The real source of your strength can be unlocked, only when you're at rock bottom. At this point, you have to figure out how to make things right again. Successful people always figure things out, even if it takes weeks, months, and years.

Being successful in life is not something for the weak hearted individual, but the strong! It takes time, and effort. There is always something we have to give in return. These truths are non-negotiable when it comes to accomplishing our dreams. A price has to be paid. You will pay in money, time, people, and even your health to be the person you want to be. One has to have a burning desire to get what they want.

The journey to success requires precision, a growth mindset, and action! I say this because two years after my game rental business crashed, I discovered another business endeavor where I was able to quadruple the income I was making as the "Game Boy King". Changing my mindset positively changed my life and these 'hacks' I will share next, will shift your life in ways you never imagined if you try them.

The Power of Frugality

As life progressed, I experienced so many wins and losses. Failure is an excellent thing, because it allows one to grow and develop the technical and analytical skills to think on their feet. With this, you can solve most problems. However, one of the biggest reasons I failed so much was that I didn't invest in my personal growth. Instead, I invested in clothes, jewelry, shoes, and excursions. I am by no means suggesting that acquiring material possession is irrelevant, but they should not be one's sole priority.

When I started to read more, I learned that systems (passive, active, and cash flow) were the keys to wealth creation. The real problem I was facing was my lack of structured systems for generating revenue or building wealth. That needed to change. The book, *Rich Dad Poor Dad*, written Robert Kiyosaki and Sharon Lechter, changed my financial mindset forever. I was ignorant of the difference between assets, liabilities, and cash flow. However, reading David Schwartz's book, *The Magic of Thinking Big,* is what changed my life completely when I learnt how to grow my mindset. His perspectives blew my mind and highlighted all the areas I needed to work on.

A huge part of my problem was comparing who I am now, to where I used to be. This left me feeling humiliated. As I read, and grew my mind, I stopped beating myself up. I was able to acknowledge that mistakes were just a part of the process. In the past, I did not have the knowledge, exposure, or mentorship needed to move past specific roadblocks. My thinking and mindset were unstable. If it was not for that, I would've been far more advanced in my endeavors. You can probably relate to this also. It has been said, "that the race is not for the swift but for the one who can endure to the end. Success is a process!

Success requires continual growth, and the moment you stop investing in yourself, I can guarantee this is when you will fail. Staying focused, blocking out distractions aids the journey. Continuously reading, researching, sharing ideas, and interacting with like- minded people is highly recommended. Napoleon Hill often said in his books *"Remaining or joining a mastermind group will give continued growth and success. But, be warned, the moment you leave, then failure knocks at your doorstep. Repetition is the mother of skill!"*

Getting what you speak!

You have to know what you want and speak it! Do not speak about what you do not wish to have, because words are potent. The Bible describes the tongue as the most powerful weapon in existence. Therefore, the level of success we have in life is directly proportional to how we speak. That being said, we can infer that words are powerful; they can do much harm, and they can do a lot of good as well. Therefore, people who want to be successful in life have to be conscious of the words they speak. Yes, it's that important! I promise you that if you talk or positively use your speech daily, your entire world will open up.

Again, the words we speak are proportional to our success! Do you agree? From the observations I've made, here's a guarantee: the more positively you speak, the greater your success! If you want to manifest all your desires, you need to have faith and believe that it will come to pass. This is very true. However, you should be realistic with your manifestations. What you desire might not come when you want it, but if you diligently have faith, execute the necessary actions to aid the process, and speak it, you'll be surprised.

Throughout my life, I have spoken what I desired. At the age of eighteen, I consistently spoke that I wanted to build, or have my own apartment. I got it! At the age of nineteen, I wanted a motorcycle: it happened! At the age of twenty, I wished for a car and business. I got them both! Can you see the recurring theme here? Remember that God is listening, and he loves you! Speak what you want into existence and eventually it will come to past.

Sometimes we are not ready or prepared to accept our manifestations. Perhaps the proper mindset isn't active, and the actions required are not being exercised correctly. For example, you cannot manifest wealth when you do not try to think, or acquire the knowledge to become a millionaire. A particular thinking pattern has to be present to be a wealthy person. One cannot expect to have children when one does not have the resources to take care of them. You cannot expect that special partner to come into your life when you are not mentally, financially, emotionally, and spiritually ready for that blessing. You have to be prepared and ready! Newton's third law of motion helps to emphasize this.

Imagine Yourself!

This mind hack is powerful! For you to be successful, you must tell yourself, and believe that you are a winner. If you do not believe in yourself, why should others believe in you? You have to have a positive self-image. Firstly, it is how you portray yourself: the clothes you wear, and your hygiene. How you look is an integral part of success. The first impression is the one that lasts the longest, and although it should not be this way, people tend to judge you based on how you look. If you carry yourself in an unkempt way, that is the impression you have given others. In contrast, if you are neatly dressed and groomed correctly with a pleasant scent, that provides a great impression. When you look after yourself in this way, it generally creates a window for opportunities. I know many factors can affect how people look, especially if they do not have the money to purchase fine clothing, or perfumes, but there is always a way. THINK! The garment does not have to be a popular brand, but what matters is how you put yourself together. Appearance matters!

Fake It Until You Make It!

Have you ever heard the saying '*You Have to Fake It Until You Make It*'. That statement can be controversial, but you have to read between the lines and understand the true meaning. This is not suggesting that you are to be a fake person, but sometimes you have to portray yourself to be something else. For example, when I started to work at the Sangster International Airport in Jamaica around age 20, I was not where I wanted to be financially. I needed capital to expand my businesses and increase my revenue. So I had to figure out a way to attract investors that I could pitch my business ideas to. Many people will not agree with the 'Fake it until you make it" concept, but I can testify that this idea has merit.

Being confident alone would not have convinced investors or managers of big organizations to invest in the business ideas I had, but mastering this craft created many opportunities. At the airport, there are many great citizens, workers, and travelers passing through every day. If you don't look or talk a particular way, no one will take you seriously, or even look at you. I was not at their level based on my status and bank account.

The conversations that I would have with the people who were considered to be in that particular 'class', would be mainly about innovation and expansions. I showed them how they would benefit from investing in my business idea and the projected profit margins. I was not intimidated. I kept my composure, and acted as though the amount of money was insignificant. Can you imagine! A young 20-year-old getting the attention of these influential people. This allowed me to "go in for the kill", and make my pitch. Eventually, I was able to acquire businesses, travel to different countries, and my co-workers at the airport spoke highly of me. That track record allowed the investors to acknowledge and take my business proposals more seriously than before. Choosing to wear some *"dope"* jewelry *"upped"* my game as well. Silver and diamond pieces were my favorites. On one occasion, I bought a nice silver plated watch with some shiny cubic stones, a bracelet and a ring also made of cubic stones – nothing too flashy though. Gold wasn't my choice because it attracted gold thieves, and I couldn't have them harassing me, or doing anything to spoil my plans.

People would always compliment me on my watch, asking me if it was real. This created the "pull" factor for me. It drew in some of the investors I wanted because people who have money are attracted by it. I looked the part, so I piqued their interest. I also knew I had to talk in a way that would display intelligence, confidence, business mindedness, and wealth. The way you speak is compelling. It can build or break you.

When I made the different pitches, I also produced the business plan with an income statement. I had a briefcase to look the part. If you want to be a successful entrepreneur or a business owner, you have to look the part and always be ready. This worked for me, and I know it can work for you too. I landed many deals and favors using this strategy. Although this strategy is very effective, at some point, you'll eventually have to evolve. Some countless programs and books are available to help you strengthen your self-image if you see yourself lacking confidence.

Faith or Fear?

Another outstanding characteristic you should build on, is faith. The lack of faith prevents many people from accomplishing their goals or unleashing their true God-given potential. This is because people are too fearful of risking it all, and do not believe in themselves. Did you know that fear is the opposite of faith, and most of the time, what we fear is on a technicality of what we think will happen? It's a non-existent attribute that infiltrates the mind with negative projections. So you have to overcome that state of mind by telling yourself that whatever you have planned will work.

Just put your all in, and if you need help, get it, but stay positive. After you do this, you will develop faith, and the more you exercise this action, the stronger your mindset becomes. You'll develop an attitude to overcome and succeed at anything you set your mind to. My mother overcame the fear of being unemployed by exercising faith in herself. As a result, her entrepreneurial pursuit gave birth creating tremendous success at a late stage in her life. I am so proud to be her son.

Chapter 2:
The People in Your Corner
Mother of the Century

In 2009, was when my mother, lost her job as housekeeping attendant. She had been working for the hotel for a significant number of years. She accumulated a lot of vacation pay that she could not collect. One day, she approached the management personnel and requested a portion of the amount to clear some debt, but was shocked to learn that she wouldn't be allowed to work while being paid out the money owed to her. She had to decide whether to continue working, or collect the vacation money owed. In this situation, she faced a very unfair request, and she had to make a tough decision.

Bills were piling up, my brother's school fees needed to be paid, and my father had issues and debt. She was in a predicament. As a result of these factors, she requested the money upfront. Unfortunately, the amount owed, though significant, was taxable. Mom gave over 14 years of her life to this establishment, and this was the thanks she got. I remember coming home from school to find her crying. It went on for days at a time, leaving our family in a sense of despair.

One day, I asked her, "what are you going to do? Are you going to look for another job or do something else?" Her reply was, "I don't know what I am going to do," with tears in her eyes. I am not an emotional person, but the feeling pierced my heart. A few days went by, until she finally came up with an idea to start a small grocery shop.

She pitched it to my father and me, and we approved. This gave her the confidence to start her own business. The money she received from her severance package was what she used as her initial startup capital. She did her market research and sourced the most frequently used items. The building was 10 x 10 square feet, and she started with three of the most popularly purchased items. She made 100% profit in her first month, and so she reinvested it into the business.

Mom repeated this process until she reached the point where she was now able to survive from the profits,. She could now use the principal amount to re-purchase stock. The business became so successful, and profitable that the profits were able to take care of the family's expenses for many years to come. Unfortunately, sometimes misfortunes have to happen for us to leave our comfort zones and discover that creative entrepreneurial side that we possess. If my mother did not go through that unfortunate situation, she wouldn't have realized she was better at being an entrepreneur than an employee.

Again, I have nothing against having a job, as we all need security and the certainty of having a steady income. Governments are trying to relinquish pension benefits, 401k accounts, and other income sources in today's economy. You have to be vigilant and watch what is happening in the market. Job security is decreasing while technology is taking over the landscape of employment.

Sooner or later, robots will be at the helm of the workforce because of their efficiency. When this becomes the norm, business owners will no longer need people. Yes, people will always be required to aid in the functionality of these machines, but how many people are studying robotics? How many robotic engineers will a business need? The economy is changing, and we need to change with it to survive.

My mom had to think of a way to solve her problems, and most entrepreneurs or successful people do as well. They think of ways to solve problems with tenacity and willpower. There will always be a challenge in life but success will be knocking at your door as long as you do not quit. When the universe pushes you, push back, and you will be surprised at the results.

They Say No! So What!

There will always be objections and rejections once you embark on the success journey. Not everyone wants to see you accomplish your goals and aspirations, because they did not get theirs, or they are just plain envious. There are many negative thinkers and evil doers (wicked people), but the onus is on you to stay focused and motivated.

Distractions and problems will be in your path, and I implore you not to avoid them but embrace them, because they will make you a stronger person. Lessons are meant to be learned.
These lessons will be through your own experience, while some from others. Dodging the process will not help you, because struggles are a requirement for someone to be successful. Once you develop the mindset to overcome and go harder, pushing day by day, you will get to where you want to be. I do not know of any successful person that has not had to deal with beating some kind of odds stacked against them.

As I am writing this book, I have to remind myself, "I know they are coming, and I am just waiting." The only thing that might throw you off is the form the obstacles present themselves in. Your greatest challenge can come from a close friend, mother, father, child, or spouse. Just be vigilant and try not to let your guard down. Seek not to play the role of victim, brush yourself off and move ahead. An important thing to note is that throughout your success journey, you will not be able to bring every one with you.

Some people are around for a reason. Some will be around only for a season, and some are there to help you achieve success. I know this might sound harsh, but it is just the truth. Whatever endeavor you embark on, people will be in your way. It hurts like a "mother fucker" (pardon my French) to go through that process. These words might bring out some emotions while reading, but it is a reality and a part of the process. Just be prepared and expect the unexpected. An important characteristic or attribute that all successful people should acquire or convey is the act of forgiveness. Forgiving someone for wrongdoing is not easy, especially if the hostile act was severe and traumatizing. However, you have to forgive even if it takes time. This will build and shape your mindset in a way you won't even believe.

Life hits me in many ways, and I had many things to work through, but I figured out how to go around the different obstacles that presented themselves. Obstacles in life come in all sorts and forms, especially with people. People can potentially be the number one obstacle you have to work with. A prime example can be illustrated when I started my second business venture at twelve years old.

After my first entrepreneurial endeavor went south, my confidence was lowered! I was trying to make extra income, and to make matters worse, whenever I asked my mother or father for money, I had to answer so many questions. They were asking to see if I really needed the money. So I have to admit, ninety-nine percent of the time, I was not successful in getting any money. Often, this made me so angry!

My father had a neighborhood friend called *Sheret*, who would often borrow movies from my father. My father had over two hundred movies in his collection, at the time. *Sheret* loved films and was so obsessed with them that she would come by the house when my father was not home to borrow a movie or two. One Monday afternoon, when I arrived home from school, and sat down to watch my favorite cartoon *Dragon Ball Z*, I heard a knock at the door. It was *Sheret* coming to borrow more DVDs from my father.

She disrupted my cartoon session, so I decided not to lend her any of the movies. Nonetheless, *Sheret* was persistent. She told me that she would pay me $300 if I gave her three films. I said, "What! Really?", she said "yes."
I asked her to return to the movies in three days. At this point, I stumbled upon my new business endeavor: "renting movies to *Sheret.*"

If I rented *Sheret* five movies each week, that would be $500 extra in my pocket. If I add the leftover money from my allowance and lunch from school, I would've accumulated $1,000 JMD each week. This was a lot of money, which meant I could buy whatever I wanted and not have to ask my parents for money. The business flourished for about three months, creating a profit of about $12,000. This was huge for a 12-year-old kid! I could feel the excitement for entrepreneurship and success flew through my veins.

It was an excellent feeling earning money like that. However, like I stated before, on the way to success, there will be obstacles. One Monday afternoon, after over three months of successful business, I came home from school and was waiting for *Sheret,* to come for her new set of DVDs. Take a guess; what happened? Instead of *Sheret* coming through the gates of the property, it was my father! Shocked by his presence, I stuttered as I greeted him. Seconds after, the gate opened again, and *Sheret* came through (I was so nervous). My father greeted her, saying,
"Hi Sheret, funny seeing you here! What do you need?" She replied saying "I'm just here returning these movies I rented from your son."

Surprised by the words coming from Sheret's mouth, my father said," What are you talking about?" "Why would Pops (my nickname) be renting you my movies?" I'm not aware of any movie renting business going on." Sheret said, "I've been renting movies for weeks now. "Dad yelled, "What!?" With a long pause and crunched face, he followed up his yell with, "Thanks for returning them, have a great day!" By the tone of my dad's voice, Sheret realized that something was wrong and quickly ran away, leaving me with my furious and hot-headed father to talk about my "new business".

The conversation with my father was a heated one! He was not happy with me, and after talking; my rental business was no more. I was devastated. You would have thought my dad would have been my biggest cheerleader. I thought he would have seen the benefits of having my own money. I was making $4000 each month, which was one sixth of his monthly salary at the time. To this day, I do not disclose how much income I make from business endeavors because it always creates some sort of issue with family or friends.

My spirit was crushed, but I said I would not give up; I had to find a way to continue my business because it gave me a sense of belonging, independence, and liberation. I also have to admit; the money was good too! It took me about two days to think of a new venture. I finally thought to myself, "Instead of renting my dad's DVD, what if I can duplicate them and have a set of my own?" I wrote down the plan, did my research, and took action.

In no time, I figured it out. At the time, I had a Dell desktop computer with a DVD-ROM burner. Based on my research, NERO Burning Studio was the software needed to go from idea to profits. Almost overnight, I was back in business! I was able to resume selling instead of renting to neighbors and friends. I doubled my income to $8000 monthly (a 100% profit margin and

2/3rd of my dad's salary). Not bad for a 12-year-old, right?

At the time, the obstacle in the way was my dad. Again, challenges came my way in all sorts of ways, but I had to be resilient and pursue my goals. Although my father was the obstacle, if he had not reacted the way he did, I would not have developed the mindset to think out of the box and figure things out. Solving the issue that presented itself created a more lucrative revenue stream for me!

To this day, I can honestly say, the entrepreneurial skills I developed came from my mother, but my survival skills came from my father. Growing up, he was not easy to deal with. As a child, he and I had many disagreements, but I thank him every day for the way he raised me. He was a disciplinarian, but he prepared me for life! I didn't learn these principles in school; I discovered them in the real world.

If you're reading this book and you still have your parents around, be grateful! They are trying to teach you valuable lessons. If you don't have your parents around, there is also a lesson there: be appreciative of life. A success mindset is very much proportional to a survival mindset. To succeed, you have to survive, and for you to survive, being successful at what you do is required. I always quote the words" Only the Strong Survive." This could not have been truer in my life at one point, so get ready as I share something to illustrate this point.

Know Your Circle!

This mind hack is one of the most potent and influential keys to an individual's success. We have to be mindful of the people we associate with or have within our circles. Our inner circle reflect who we are, or who we want to be. If someone doesn't know who you are personally, they usually judge you based on the people you associate with. There is a saying that says "birds of a feather flock together."

The choice is yours to decide who you want to be around. There are specific characteristics a successful person has. It is either you will emit negative energy, or positive energy. If an individual associate him/herself with negative people, they will eventually develop a negative mindset without even knowing! Success with a negative attitude doesn't work.

A negative mindset is when you focus on the negative side of others, experiences and situations. You want to stay as far away as possible from harboring negative energy. I implore you always to be mindful of your associations. It has been so helpful to have the right people around me. However, there have been times when I have had the wrong people around, and I've lived to regret it. Journey with me to a time I was "locked up".

Locked Up

It was August 2013 when I decided to make more money by starting a bike rental business. I had started three businesses that were profitable, and was expanding to the fourth. Remember, AGE HAS NO BOUNDARIES! I was 20 at the time. No matter how young or old you are, you can be very successful in business with the right mindset and work ethics! You have to learn the process of scaling and expansion.

Start with the idea, take action and eliminate age-bound excuses. The reason I chose to start a motorcycling rental business was that opportunity was knocking! The famous DREAM WEEKEND and ATI parties were being held in Negril, near my hometown. The parties had a global presence! People worldwide flew into the country just to enjoy these parties, and mainly used motorcycles to get around.

The area was too congested for the use of cars. Motorcycles were perfect for getting around. Travelers acquired loans from banks and friends to have that experience! So I came up with a great way to put myself in a position to earn income from the large influx of traffic. Many tourists would be flaunting their money, spending it on dancing, drinking, and partying on another level. Who would not want a piece of the pie?

Typically, the cost to rent motorcycles would be $1000.00 JMD per day. However, during that period, the

Small Boy Big Profits

price would skyrocket to $5000.00JMD. That's a 500% profit! Another income generator was operating *motorcycle taxis* with the motorcycles. We would charge around $100 per trip. During the *Dream weekend period,* it would rapidly increase to about $600JMD. We were also able to get tips, so this was a fantastic time for me to get into the business. At the time, I owned only one motorcycle. So, I had to get another one quickly, and at an affordable rate, if I was to make a profit. I visited a few dealers, but they increased their prices because of the weekend, which put a massive obstacle in my path. I had to figure out a way to get one!

Having so many successes at a young age, I was known on the streets as "The Young Money Maker." It was sad, but the success and money got to my head. I started bragging to my friends about how lavishly I was living. I began to spend large amounts of money on drinks at parties, jewelry, and expensive technology. To make matters worse, I associated with people who would flaunt how much money they had as well. I was not humble at all, and as a result, I was struck by a tragedy that summer.

I couldn't get a second motorcycle, and it led me to try to take a shortcut. I was asking mechanics in and around the town if they had any bikes available. I searched diligently for a seller until I came across two young men in the neighborhood who said they could help me find a cheap bike. As time began to run out, my eagerness and greed blocked my judgment. I was conducting business with two strangers that I did no background check on, and I blindly trusted them. The two men told me to get the money and meet them back at the spot that I had found them.

When I returned, they were there waiting for me. One guy said they would escort me to where the motorcycle was being held, and I'd pay there. They then told me that they would make a quick stop at their home on the way. I did not even think about what was being said! All I could think about were the profits that were going to be made. I made two huge mistakes in this situation: 1) trusting strangers and 2) going alone.

On my way there, the path was very dark, so one of the men suggested taking a shortcut, and I promptly said yes." I thought to myself, "the faster we reached our destination, the better". My eager attitude was indeed at its peak! Suddenly, the car stopped abruptly, and the men quickly fled the vehicle, and two men armed with guns approached the vehicle! I can still hear them saying, "This is a robbery; give us the money now." I tried to distract them by spreading the money over the vehicle, but I wasn't successful. They said," if you move, I will shoot." I was so traumatized and shocked, I just cooperated and gave them the money, so they didn't harm me.

I was robbed of one hundred and fifty Jamaican Dollars, along with my cellular phone, wallet, and business credit cards. This situation was all due to impatience and greed. It was a tragic moment, but I was so grateful to be alive because the situation could have been a lot worse. I made it back home safely, however, I did not tell any of my friends or family what had happened. I was too scared, ashamed, and disappointed in myself.

The morning after, my mother woke me up in a fit because she was receiving many calls. She asked me what I did the night before and went on to explain that she just gotten a phone call from a police officer stating that they discovered my wallet at a crime scene!" I gasped for air as I tried to explain my innocence. I was summoned to turn myself in for questioning. All I could ask was What?" "Really!"

Upon arriving at the police station, I identified myself and told them why I was there. The officer in charge said, "young man, we found your wallet at a robbery crime scene, and we will have to hold you until we can verify what happened."

I told him what had happened that night and declared my innocence. The officer ignored my comments, but I knew he was just following protocol, and just like that, I ended up in jail for something I did not do. The people who robbed me, had robbed more people that night and threw my wallet away. The wallet was later found by an officer, making me a suspect! During the holding process, I was placed in a cell with six criminals who committed serious crimes such as murder, theft, and sexual assault.

My reputation was on the line, and I was at the mercy of the inmates. I spent two days in a jail cell but was released, harm-free, with no criminal record. Thank God for that, as it could have been a different story! While in the cell, I learned many lessons from the inmates: some of their struggles and why they committed those crimes.

Even in a jail cell, you have rules and regulations to follow, or the consequences can be very severe. My eyes were also opened to the fact that not everyone who ends up in prison or jail is always guilty. Many were just in the wrong place at the wrong time. The two days I was locked up showed me who was a genuine friend and who wasn't. In my "paparazzi moment, "I was able to feel how movie stars felt when going through scandals. It taught me to be careful who I do business with, associate with, and call friends. I also learned not to be greedy but rather be patient and humble.

After experiencing such a horrible experience, I always strive to conduct legitimate business deals. I experienced being in a cell with "The Crazy Outlaws" (5 High Profile Criminals). After having this crazy time, who wouldn't be changed, right? Money, wealth, or fame shouldn't control you; rather you should be in control of it! This experience showed me the power of the law of attraction. Success attracts more success, abundance, wealth, but it can also attract people with bad intentions. Know your circle!

Chapter 3:
Stack Your Businesses Before Your Cash
Good Friends Are Better Than Pocket Money

During my time at the AJAS Aviation services (Sangster's International Airport, Jamaica), I met some fantastic people. Perhaps the most influential was a woman named Sudha Higgins. Sudha was not only beautiful, but she had a heart of gold. She was a supervisor for the United Airlines fleet.

One Wednesday afternoon, as I headed back to the main office, to file some paperwork for a Condor Flight I had just done, I overheard Ms. Higgins complaining about her issues she was having with her cellular phone. I stopped and offered to help her. At the time, I had a small phone-sales and repair business. After asking her what the issue was, she said, "This phone is stressing me out." I can't make any calls, and this screen is flickering every time I touch it!"

I took the cellphone and was able to quickly diagnosed the problem. I gave her two solutions: she could either or reset the phone back to the factory settings, or change the phone's touch sensor pad. She said she did not have the time or energy to go in town to fix it.

After seeing her frustration, I offered to fix it for her free of charge; I saw how upset and frustrated she was about the situation. She said," thank you so much I appreciate it." As business people, we ought always to show acts of kindness, expecting nothing in return. So I did as I promised. She was very grateful.

This small gesture forged a great friendship between us. Later down the road, Sudha was also kind to me by showing me how to do my job right, giving good advice, and helping me excel within the company. The business advice she gave me paved the way to landing high-ranking investors for the different business endeavors I started. Associating myself with her, boosted my image and the quality of people in my circle. Sudha was also influential in my getting into the Sunwing Flight Attendant Program. This was the opportunity of a lifetime.

Sunwing Airlines needed a person who lived in Jamaica to operate as a flight attendant. This I suppose would prevent canceled and delayed flights caused by injury or temporarily incapacitated crewmembers. I applied for the Flight attendant program and was chosen. This was incredible for me because, under normal circumstances, positions like these are not readily available. In addition, I traveled to multiple cities at the Airline's expense, for I was the only flight attendant based in Jamaica at the time.

Working as an attendant was an incredible opportunity, and without Sudha's influence and encouragement, it might not have happened. Another opportunity that became available was when she migrated to Canada. She didn't have anyone to take over her Stocking business. In addition to my entrepreneurial pursuits and working for AJAS Aviation Services as a customer service representative, I was elated to have the opportunity to add Sudha's Stocking business venture to my portfolio. The opportunity allowed me to capitalize on another revenue stream. Yet again, I saw the power of kindness, and having the right persons in my circle.

Do you see the Big Profits? They came in many forms. Life has a funny way of rewarding us. Demonstrating acts of kindness, generosity, and being selfless can generate tremendous benefits. These benefits can come from the people we surround ourselves with.

Think Big

Do you believe that what you picture is what manifests into your universe? What you think about is what you will get. This thought needs to be deeply considered. In my experience, your aspirations and goals in life are solely dependent on you. If you put in the necessary work, remain dedicated, take risks, and acquire the knowledge you need, your life can change. While pursuing your desires, obstacles and distractions will appear. Do not give up! Grow your mindset and remain focused.

Throughout my career as an entrepreneur, I can honestly say I often gave into distractions, was stressed often, and lost money. It is only human for someone to take losses, but it is what you do afterwards that counts! Many people let failure stop them, but embrace failure and prepare for it because it will only make you stronger. It will also heighten your focus. Who knows, you might even surprise yourself during the process.

I say this because I surprised myself! I had doubts when I started a business venture selling hair extensions. During the market research phase, I talked to people in, and out of the industry. I received mainly negative feedback. Some people even said that the market is too saturated and I won't make it, but for some reason, it didn't discourage me at all. Instead, it fueled and piqued my curiosity because I saw the revenue and potential profits. So, although the point of entry was unclear and unpredictable, I still took the risk!

Hair Business

It was in September of 2015 when I began implementing the next business idea. I entered the beauty industry (particularly selling hair extensions). Life was going well for me. I had a great job at Sangster's International Airport, and the DVD sales and rental businesses were going well. The electronics sale, and repair business was also very profitable - beyond what I could imagine. However, it felt monotonous. It wasn't that I wasn't grateful for the amount of profits I was making, but there was a feeling of stagnation which overpowered and hit me very deeply.

I said to myself, "What is going on, Garnet? You need to increase your revenue streams; You are not going to be a millionaire with these businesses alone!" "Garnet, get a hold of yourself and start thinking!" At that moment, I realized that people could self-motivate themselves. They have the power to think about the situation they are in and where they want to be. I motivated myself and started researching for a new opportunity that would increase my income tremendously.

I analyzed the different markets and searched for various trends in my location. I did this for three months and discovered that women spent more money than men, and that is the market I should target. I also learned that females spent theirs and their partners' money. I had discovered that women's spending habits are greatly influenced by the perceptions they think their peers have of them, and the opinions of society about their appearance. I had a great opportunity in my hand.

First, I started thinking about selling women's clothing, but I realized that the profit margins were not that high, especially if you are not well-known. Brand recognition and good marketing are what fuel the clothing industry. I needed a product that not only had good profit margins, remarkable shelf life but was loved by women. I articulated my desires into the atmosphere. I believed that there must be a product that could get me the results that I needed.

One Sunday afternoon, as I headed home from work, my eyes stumbled on this fine beautiful young lady. I'd say that she was beyond beautiful, but what caught my eyes was the length of her hair. It was long and dazzling. I believe it was about thirty inches in length where I said to myself," that extension has to cost a lot of money." I immediately pulled out my phone, and started googling the cost of hair extensions according to the length, and the results struck me. I had discovered my winning product!

When I arrived home, I researched more to see how much the product cost, the profit margin I could make, who the suppliers were, and ways to get the product. The results were incredible; I saw profit margins of up to 400%. I reached out to a few suppliers and those with the best prices located in China. I was skeptical because I would be sending money to someone in China who I have never met! What made it even more difficult was that shipping was not directly to Jamaica at the time.

Doubt, fear, and disappointment were the emotions taking over my body because this was a huge risk, and I had terrible experiences in the past dealing with strangers. Nevertheless, the opportunity was on my mind all day and night, and as a result, I was restless at work the next day. At work, I asked a few women for their opinions. Most of them indicated that they would spend money on extensions because of how it makes them look – appearances! They also shared how they got their hair extensions and the customs fees associated. I knew I could solve this issue and get their business.

As entrepreneurs or successful people, when problems present themselves, we solve the issue. I knew there must be a way I can get these hair extensions. It could not be that hard, so I researched and discovered that if I send the item to the U.S.A. instead of Jamaica, the shipping time would be less, and there wouldn't be a huge customs fee. With the shipping and customs fee issue now solved, I had to figure out how to get them in Jamaica. A thought came to my mind: I should send the items to someone in the USA, who also would be travelling to Jamaica. This would alleviate the customs fee and shipping time. I reached out to a few friends, but most of them turned me down, except one friend,

Sabrina (nickname-Emay) . I told her my idea and she agreed to help deliver the hair extensions when returning to the country.

After talking to Sabrina, I breathed a sigh of relief. The only obstacle in my way was taking the risk of purchasing in China. I was in too deep and couldn't turn back now, so I took the risk of sending two hundred thousand Jamaican dollars via PayPal to the supplier. My heart skipped a beat when the money was credited from my bank account. Seven days later, Sabrina told me that she received the products; this was music to my ears.

She returned to the country two days after, and I received the products with no delays or customs fees. When I received the products, I started marketing and distribution right away. The revenue I made within the first month was enormous, and the products were a *hot* commodity. To my amazement, I made more than the 400% profit margin I was predicting. I made a profit of One and a half Million Jamaican dollars in my first month. I had never made such a huge amount of money before, in such a short period!

This greatly improved the quality of my life. The income I generated aided in purchasing my first car - a Mitsubishi Lancer. I was also able to expand my other businesses. I do believe that if you have a business idea or a goal, pursue it, because you might just surprise yourself in the same manner I did. Life is like a chess game; you have to move very strategically, be focused, and be determined to win. There will always be setbacks, moments of fear, doubt, discouragement from peers and family, but once you know the reason and take action, nothing will stop you from succeeding. Tenacity, faith, and a risk-taking mindset are the keys to winning!

(Mom and Dad If you are reading this, I apologize for not disclosing my financial earnings with you back then - smiles)

Sometimes, it is not best to disclose all your financial earnings because it may cause problems between family members, friends, or even a spouse.

Mentorship

When I hear the word mentorship, there are many questions that come to my mind: Who should be a mentor? What qualities should he/she possess? Why should someone listen to such a person? The simple answer is that a mentor is in a position in life where you want to be, or have the formula you need. Often, you might not have direct access to these persons, so another way of receiving mentorship that I recommend, is listening to the published work of these experts: video recordings, following them on social media sites like Instagram or Facebook, or even accessing materials through platforms like YouTube. These are some of the best ways to absorb and learn the lessons being taught. I listen to a lot of audio recordings from various people. I need their wisdom and strength. This is one of my top recommendations in growing your mindset.

Betrayal

The process of being very successful will not be easy, and many unexpected events will happen. Some will be so nerve-wracking that we will never forget, and it may scar us for life. Let me clarify a little more: As we ride along the success train, we have certain people in our circle. We tend to believe that everyone is on the train for the same purpose, which is not always the case. Some people will have to be left behind, especially if they do not share the same vision as you. These individuals may do things that hurt, prevent or slow down your progress. What is most unexpected is who the individual(s) are. They can be close friends, relatives, mother, father, lover, husband, wife, you name it. Don't let betrayal take you out.

Time Management

This success quality is crucial because time is a commodity that cannot be regained, and one should always strive to use it wisely. As people who want to be successful, or are on the way to success, we have to know where and with whom our time is spent. The people you spend time with can predict how far our success will go. Working harder and smarter without the proper time management skills will result in failure. Distractions will come, and we have to see them coming from a mile away! Distractions can come in many forms. To be successful entrepreneurs and professionals, you have to know how to identify them. They can be a new job opportunity, social media (THE REAL KILLER), promotions, mergers, even more sales. A close friend of mine would always say, "Chambers, not every opportunity is an opportunity; you have to analyze each one carefully to see if it fits your portfolio." This proved true right down to the point of me writing this book. In the middle of trying to complete the writing of this book, I experienced many delays, emotional stress, and mental hurdles, but I overcame them to move forward.

Distractions can also come from relationships - hanging with friends or family members on multiple excursions, parties, or events. I am by no means diminishing the important task of enjoying one's life, but one must keep abreast of the frequency, and reduce it if it becomes excessive! Working on your goals and dreams does not come easy, and if you want high-level results, then a certain amount of effort has to be over the top at times. Our ultimate level of success is determined by certain habits, and even people who we associate with. It might be hard to believe, but taking incremental steps will help the process until people no longer have hold over you.

The success journey is a sacrificial one, and the change has to be accurate because no one can expect results when wasting time. If one continues to do the same things, in the same way all the time, you will always get the same results. Everyone has 24 hours in a day, and what you do with your time during those hours will determine your level of success. Remember, time lost can never be regained, so use it very wisely.

The Ultimate Power: Focus

For one to be successful in any endeavor, he or she has to focus. This is the only way for your goal to be achieved. Billionaire Warren Buffet said that if anyone has many businesses, they should limit the focus down to three 3 areas. I agree we should focus on one thing at a time. Think about it; most students are not given more than a few courses to complete at a time in school. You do not graduate until you can show that you can master one level and move to the next, completing all the courses given, not just one. We have to have the same mindset in business.

But the question is if it is possible to have multiple companies and succeed? Society condemns the jack-of-all-trades mentality, but can anyone really name a billionaire who has just one business? That will be tough, because millionaires and billionaires engage in multiple pursuits in an attempt to generate STREAMS of income. When one has numerous companies, the time will come to scale them, and you scale one business at a time, so you can have laser focus. Once you scale one, start the other; therefore, I believe it is ok for anyone to start multiple businesses simultaneously. However, the scalability aspect is when someone should make a single focus.

Consider this! When I should have been laser-focused during the writing process, a job opportunity presented itself with an excellent salary attached to it. The job was to be a district supervisor for a popular restaurant franchise. The opportunity was irresistible because they offered a "whopping" sixty-five thousand Canadian dollar salary, per annum. I accepted the offer and proceeded to carrying out the duties that were required of me. About two weeks in, I realized that I was overworked due to multiple issues. I was also multitasking in order to ensure smooth operations: cooking, serving, managing new teams, training new staff, and ensuring they followed proper inventory procedures.

To top it all off, I had only one day off each week; the job was demanding. It reached a point where my health was in jeopardy, and I had to decide whether to continue working, or lose out on that incredible salary. At the time, I had to pause all my other jobs in order to focus on the job at hand. That was a big mistake, as eventually, I had to quit the job. I had no income coming in for about two weeks. I also had no time to write because of the exhaustive process.

While I was working, I lost focus of my goal (writing this book), and I almost lost my other sources of income. This situation showed me that one must analyze opportunities that present themselves; weighing both the pros and the cons. If I had not developed a resilient mindset, failure and loss would have been the result, but tenacity allowed me to bounce back quickly. I was able to pivot back to where I should be. Being focused is very important because one wrong move can cost you dearly.

Diversify or Die!

Having the chance to travel to the U.S.A. was one of my greatest successes in life, and I think most people who came from a third-world country would say the same. To travel to the US, you have to apply for a visa, which at times is not always easy to acquire. The first time I applied for that visa, I was denied, but I never gave up! I couldn't give up because of the available opportunities. I exercised patience and took action to get the necessary requirements.

Thankfully, eight months after reapplying, I was successful. The United States is deemed the land of opportunity because of the economic opportunities, the quality of life you can experience if you work hard, and the countless business opportunities that exists. Having a USA visa enhanced my business profits because It allowed the elimination of third-party expenses. In addition, I was now able to handle products directly for all of my businesses. As a result, I expanded my companies and traveled to more cities giving me more exposure to different contexts.

Finally, I was able to enjoy the revenues I had made! If I needed to relax a bit, I could simply catch a flight to Florida, or wherever my mind desired. Life was perfect, and the possibilities were endless, even scary at times! I encourage everyone to become an entrepreneur because it allows you the freedom to make decisions when you want to make them, to do what you want to do, when you want to. You are your own boss! By this time, I had earned approximately three hundred thousand Jamaican dollars as my monthly net salary - a long way from where I started!

Revealing this information right now will shock some of my relatives and friends because no one knew of my earnings. However, I choose to disclose this information because if I was able to make it amidst all the different obstacles in a third-world country, of course, you could make it too whether you reside in America, Canada, UK, Caribbean, wherever! You have to put that work in, master your craft and eliminate complacency. If you do not stay focused, you might lose what you are working assiduously to accomplish. All the concepts and revenue-generating streams mentioned in this book are still operational today.

As time went on, I traveled more, and I was enjoying my life in the USA. The exposure was so addictive! I decided that I would migrate to the USA because the possibilities were better and I could enhance my life tremendously. The people I associated with, and maintaining the lifestyle of my family were important to me. I had to figure out how to generate income in the same way, and even more while maintaining my businesses and my own needs. Although business was perfect for me, I grew weary of just sticking to the Jamaican economy. It felt monotonous and I needed a change. I made a few connections and spoke with people

I had met while traveling in the USA. I wanted to know what it takes to live in America.

One of my co-workers introduced me to a friend he met who was also a business owner. I was able to get some guidance from him as to how to proceed with migrating to the U.S. He indicated that he could *'hook me up'* with a business opportunity that would help me get started when I got there." I would earn around $6,000 U.S. dollars monthly (net).

Earning that amount, in addition to my side businesses would give me a total monthly income of about $10,000 U.S. Dollars (net). I had no more questions, America here I come! Financial freedom here I come! I was so enthusiastic about the potential possibilities that I started to liquidate all the assets that I had accumulated in Jamaica. I even liquidated my passive income streams, just to be more than prepared.

It turned out that it was a mistake to liquidate everything I had. I usually take calculated risks, but out of excitement, I did not fully prepare this time. I told myself I would take the risk because if I made it in a third-world country, why wouldn't I make it in a first-world country. I spoke what I believed. Reflecting now, I think I was overly confident. Little did I know that I was in for the ride of my life, making this transition.

No storm can stop me!

On the day of my flight, there came the category five hurricane Irma. I gasped for air when I heard the information on the news. Immediately, I called the airline to inquire about the status of the flight. The Airline told me that my scheduled flight was the last one leaving. This was music to my ears because not even a hurricane was going to stop me from accomplishing my dreams; I had to get to the U.S.A. Southwest Airlines was indeed the best.

As we all waited with baited breath at the airport, one could see the huge dark cumulus clouds soaring over the coastal waters. I was so determined to go. I ignored mom's warnings. It was too late to turn back now, so I boarded the flight, and off it went! While in the sky, the pilots diverted from the regular route, and something unique caught my eye; I saw the sky split in two. One side had the sun and bright white clouds, and the other side had a dark, scary appearance with lightening and thunderclaps which could be felt in the aircraft.

As we approached America, there was turbulence. It was like driving on a bumpy road with twists and turns. To make matters worse, other travelers started to panic. The normal route to travel would be on the east coast of Florida, going around Cuba, through the Atlantic, but we went through the Gulf of Mexico. The pilots chose this way for a safer trip, but it was bumpy. Nonetheless, we landed safely. After clearing customs and immigration, I went to the arrivals section, looked up in the air, I said, "Nothing can stop me now!"

The Twist

When I arrived and got settled, I reached out to the person who I was to meet. I called him but was unsuccessful until two days later. He gave me what I needed to get started. I did as instructed and would later appear at a car dealership. The contact there was confused by my presence.

I told him who referred me, and what I was told to do. To my surprise, he told me that I must be mistaken and he didn't know who, or what I was referring to. I immediately reached out to my contact and explained what had happened. I was in for more disappointment when he told me that he did not have any personally connections with the owners, but was just trying to help me out; the persons must have changed their minds. An argument had developed between us because he did not deliver on his end of the deal. I was upset.

I sold everything I had to take up this opportunity, and it fell through! I thought that all he was giving me were excuses. Eventually, the connection between him and I ended, and I had to find a way to survive. Going back to Jamaica wasn't an option for me, because not only would it be very embarrassing, but I had nothing to go back to! The situation put me in a state of depression because thinking about how hard and long I worked to be where I was, to lose everything in a couple of days was, disappointing, and just very stressful.

I had no way to earn an income, and my cash reserves were dwindling day by day. What an awful position I had found myself in! Weeks passed, and there were no opportunities. I cried and prayed to God for a breakthrough every day. Finally, a thought came to my mind that I should probably try calling petrol stations or restaurants because these establishments are more likely to be hiring.

I reached out to a few petrol stations and a few restaurants, inquiring if there were any vacant positions available, and all I got were disappointing responses. Oh, the disappointment I felt! I began to lose hope! I got on my knees and started praying again. After I finished praying, I got back up and started calling different businesses.

I continued making calls and one business owner, gave a positive response, and asked about my experience. I told her I could do just about anything. The person immediately replied, "well, maybe this isn't the place for you." Immediately, I interrupted her and asked if I could come to talk in person. She told me to come in, and I wasted no time!

I got dressed, found the address, and proceed for an interview. I made sure I was well dressed because I know that people judge you by the way you look. When

I arrived, I was interviewed and asked if I could start immediately. While at the restaurant, I was escorted to the kitchen at the sink area and was given the job of washing dishes. I was very grateful for the opportunity because this would allow me to make some money. But then, reality hit me, and I realized that I lost everything and had to start from ground zero.

The Come Back

I said to myself: "Is this what I have been reduced to?" "I had a good customer service job at the Airport, was a part-time flight attendant, had businesses was making enough money, and now I'm a pot washer? (I mean no offense to those who do this for a living) Nonetheless, I swallowed my pride, pressed forward, and adapted to the new situation. I did this job for two months, but I talked with the staff members, customers, and even the owner about my story. As time progressed, I got promoted from washing dishes, to cooking, then to serving customers. My duties then evolved from catering orders to fixing the glitches in the Point of Sales (POS) system. From there, I was delivering food to other locations, and even managed some of the money. At that point, I believed that I had gained the trust and confidence of the store owner and the staff.

In the space of four months, I went from dishwasher to an indirect assistant store manager. With the money made, I was able to reinvest into the Hair Extension business I had started a while back. I sent resources back home in Jamaica to my girlfriend to restart operations. The hair extension business was up and running again.

With my confidence reignited, I wanted to do things right. I was able to get my ITIN number to file taxes with the IRS. No one wishes the IRS to be knocking on their doorstep asking how and why things are not reported. Uncle Sam wants his piece of the pie, and you do not want your business to go down because of mismanagement of taxes. In five months, I made five figures; I worked incredibly long hours at the restaurant, created websites for small businesses, and cleaned people's houses, businesses, stadiums. I did what was necessary to survive. I lost everything and got it back because I chose not to give up.

An opportunity knocked on my door to go to Canada to finish school. The tuition to attend Sheridan College was about USD 16,000 a year, which was a lot of money for me! I knew it would be a grind, but I had to figure it out as my time in the states was closing. After learning, I could split my tuition payments. I was relieved because I did not want to put all my earnings into school. I generated more than USD 20,000 in those five months from all of my jobs and business ventures!

This was another step to my BIG PROFITS; can you see it? I'm convinced it was my determination, tenacity, faith in God, and the willpower to succeed amidst failure, that pivoted me back on the right path. If I could do it, you can too. A positive mindset and action are what it takes. The way to success will never be comfortable. Avoid the temptation to stay in your comfort zone. Diamonds are made under pressure so if you want to be one, get ready for the journey. #Only The Strong Survive!

Chapter 4:

The Third Time's a Charm?

As I continued on my entrepreneurial journey, I got the chance to migrate to Canada and further my education. Canada has excellent health care systems, and a better culture of acceptance towards immigrants. Although I was alone in the country with no family, attending school in Canada allowed me to study while working. To say that I felt motivated would be an understatement. I felt empowered! I have worked extremely hard to get to this point!

While at Sheridan College, I enrolled in the Computer and Software Engineering program. The winter season in Canada were very cold, and this affected me greatly, considering that I was from the sunny island of Jamaica. With temperatures dropping as low as minus thirteen degrees Celsius, I was often uncomfortable, but this was the price I had to pay. None-the-less, amidst the cold weather, I enjoyed my classes. My professors were caring.

The school atmosphere was terrific, and to top it off, mingling with people from different ethnicities, learning about their culture was very intriguing. I loved the new life I had, mainly because I excelled in all my courses with very high grades. Everything was going according to plan until about twelve weeks into the program I was informed that I would need to pay the remaining portion of my tuition in order to continue my studies. It caught me by surprise because I thought I had paid for half of the year.

I contacted the international students' department and told them they had to have made a mistake. I eventually met with the department head, who explained that I had only paid for one semester, which is the equivalent of twelve weeks. I thought the fifty percent tuition I paid was for six months when it was really for three months. How could I have overlooked such a crucial detail? This happens a lot when one gets overly excited about new opportunities.

At that point, I had to figure out a way to come up with the money to pay for the rest of the tuition. When I checked my accounts, I realized that I was nowhere near the amount needed. The money I had left, was mainly to help support me with living expenses and with basic amenities. I had to pool all the money I had in both offshore and inland accounts to aid the situation. Yet still, the money was nowhere enough. The part that hurt the most was that I had to stop all business operations because of this predicament.

There it was again, losing because of my ignorance. Immediately I became stressed, and depression was now knocking at my doorstep. The dreams and goals I had were now smashed to pieces! I had two options: either to take all the money I had accumulated and go back home to Jamaica, or spend what I had until I found a way out. I chose the latter.

Survival Mode

I could not see a way out at all. I prayed, meditated, and asked God for a way out. I can truly say with confidence that prayer works! You may not get your answer when you want it, but keep praying, you will get your answer when you need it. The answer from above was diversification. For me to survive, I needed to diversify and stretch myself! So I looked for two jobs to supplement my income. It would put a strain on my health; but I had to be resilient and push as hard as I could, while going to school.

This was hard-core pressure, especially with the weather conditions. I worked for a warehouse where I packed boxes on the overnight shift. The second job was at a restaurant where I worked as a chef. In between these jobs, I would attend classes from noon to 8:00 pm. I was miserable, frustrated, and just unhappy at times. As each day went by, the struggle and stress became unbearable. I was going through a lot.

There were times when I had no place to sleep. So I slept in my car, and lived below my means. I can vividly remember how I almost lost the toes on my right foot because of how cold it was one night. I had traveled in the snow to meet Joni (a cousin-in-law I learned I had in Canada), to ask about an apartment for rent. It was worth it, because she allowed me to live with her. I had to leave school to manage it all, but I was NOT going back home.

Out of the Box Thinking

While out of school, I went to different professional development trainings to gain more skills. One of these, was to become trained in operating forklift machines. It paid well and was one of the highest positions in the warehouse. I passed the training exams and applied to different temporary agencies afterward. This worked until some companies needed five years of experience, which I didn't have. So the season of the warehouse was short-lived.

I went back to the drawing board and applied for different jobs online. I got accepted for a few, but I choose three. The first job was for a cleaning company to sweep and mop department offices, and factory buildings. The second job was as a dishwasher at a restaurant, and the third was a forklift position. I worked all three!

The cleaning company was my gig on the weekends, and the others were on weekdays. I made about two thousand Canadian dollars per week, but I was trading my time for money, which means no social life. I can surely tell you this new way of life was not comfortable, but I had to survive. Often, I reached out to my parents asking for some advice as to what to do. This made them sad at times, and they wanted me to come home, but I was determined, and confident that I would make it back on my feet.

My mother advised me to try finding a local church to attend so I could get a sense of hope, and some spiritual help. So I did as I was told, and found the Mississauga SDA church. Here is where I found people who were loving, well-mannered, professional, and caring. They encouraged me to trust in God, have faith, believe, and manifest my dreams and desires to God. Words are potent.

Some people took me in like family, provided me with food, and gave good advice. This was truly powerful beyond measure! So, again, surround yourself with great people! Attending that church was one of the best decisions that I ever made because the information I received blessed my life. My hope and vision grew even more robust, which restored my confidence.

After being exposed to different resources, I realized my mindset was not how it should be. I was thinking like an unsuccessful person. I wanted to be rich, but I was not thinking as the wealthy does. There are certain habits of mind that are common amongst the wealthy; we can all learn and adapt them. Everyone can be successful. The challenge is that many are ignorant of the many mindset hacks available.

"The Magic of Thinking Big" changed my life forever. It helped me see the value of my life and accept that life will never be easy. So much of life is how you react to a given situation. Being focused, tenacious, and resilient, will give you the ammunition to succeed in life. Your mindset is what matters!

Changing my mindset gave me the willpower to not focus on my struggles and hardships but to focus on my goals. In fact, I was able to later re-establish my businesses, and create new ones. My NiQy Hair Brand was given life again. Not only that, I also birthed NiQy Cleaning Services, and NiQy Care Services. I approached six figures in Canada with these business ventures. I also started a company where I specialized in website creation, enhancements, and optimization for clients who sought to market their products online (Jr Marketing Help Inc.) while still holding down my regular job.

This book serves not to discourage anyone from having a" nine to five" job because we need that seed money to fuel our side businesses until they take off. I am also not just saying that success looks only like exotic cars, houses, and material possessions. Primarily, I'm focused on the mindset of an individual. Once you have the correct mindset, wealth, money, and success, (in whatever shape or form), will come your way. Revenue generation is connected to how you think. Trust me, I know.

Chapter 5:
You Are the Answer

Have you ever wondered why your life is the way it is right now? What would you say is the solution to solving the problems and struggles life throws at you? Ninety percent of us would say, 'the lack of money'. If that is your answer, you need to think deeper, because money alone will not make your life better. Mastering the way, you think is what I believe makes your life better. I say this because if you do not have the correct thinking or mindset, even when you accumulate more money, your problems may not go away; in fact, they might increase!

Have you ever heard the quote, "the more money you make, the more problems are created? Why is this statement true? I say, lack of financial literacy and discipline. What is the solution? You are, of course! Ignorance is one of the root causes of many issues people have today. It is crucial to be wise. Seek wisdom! I challenge you to get financial wisdom.

The first step is to start reading books about wealth because many successful people show you the blueprint of how they created, managed, and built wealth. If that is your principal issue in life, then that's where you should start. The solution to any issue or problem you have, is in a book somewhere! People love to share their experiences. Sadly, many people do not like to read because it might not be fun, entertaining or whatever excuse they come up with. I also was a victim of this mindset.

Thankfully, I came to the realization that the successful and wealthy people of this world were readers. So I had to develop the habit of reading. I can vividly remember that it took me five years to complete the reading of the book *"Twilight New Moon."* If you genuinely want to be successful, then you have to study what successful people do. You cannot say you want to be successful, if you are doing the same things you've been doing for the past five years. Change starts with the way you think.
 There is another thought that says, 'As you think, so you become!' If you think ambitiously, then you will become successful. If you think optimistically, then you achieve your goals. Negative thinking breeds negative results. The way the mind works is truly unique, and you have to protect it because your greatest ideas lie there.

With the proper mental programming, you can become a different person in time. You will learn how to better handle struggles and hard times. You might ask, where are the solutions? I would say you are the answer! All the solutions lie within you.

Now that you are aware of the mindset you must have, let's talk about the things you can do to skyrocket your revenues! It begins with getting control of your money.

Chapter 6:
Getting Out of Debt

When we spend more than our income, we are often forced to acquire loans, and may even mismanage the money we have earned. Debt eventually chokes us. Throughout my career, I racked up a lot of debt: credit cards, bank loans, loans from family friends - I had done it all! You probably can relate to some of these examples. When I lived in Jamaica, my debt ratio became very meager; if I needed an item, I had to have the cash upfront to get what I wanted. So, I learned how to delay gratification.

When I migrated to America/Canada, because the system was more open to giving out loans, accessing money was much easier. Delayed gratification was not always necessary. For example, when someone first immigrates to Canada, they usually start with a good credit score, generally around 690 points. This puts individuals in a good position to access cash loans; immigrants generally make good use of such opportunities. Who would not want access to "easy money"?

When I landed in Canada, I *hopped* on every opportunity that presented itself. I had four credit cards, took out countless number of loans, bought high-end electronics, furniture, and the list goes on. Anything my heart desired at the time, I purchased. Little did I know that this move would come to haunt me later in my life. In six months, I was in debt as high as five figures. I was not accustomed to this way of life. I had 'maxed out' my credit cards and was way over my loan limits. Consequently, the late fees and the interest I had accumulated, was adding insult to injury. Having bad credit makes life very difficult! So I knew I had to figure out how to increase my credit rating and get rid of all, or at least most of the accumulated debt. I knew I needed help, so I sought the advice of a few financial advisors. Much to my disappointment, they did not have any concrete ideas to help me reduce my debt quickly. This forced me to think outside of the box in order to come up with a workable solution.

I remembered reading the book *Rich Dad Poor Dad*, where the author talked about using good debt to clear up bad debt. This advice inspired me to approach different payday institutions to sign up for loans. I then used them to pay off the debt that had been impacting my credit. This was crucial in building my credit rating. It took me about three months to pay back the pay day loans; becoming loan free and bad debt free.

Another approach I have tried is borrowing money from close relatives and friends. This can be tricky because you still have to show your ability to repay, even though you are borrowing from people you know! In my case, I approached a few associates of mine, and proposed a ten percent overall interest on a loan amount. This was a win-win. I was able to reduce my debt-to-income ratio.

You can also access online courses that offer advice to reduce debt, and for turning credit into cash. However, it is important to conduct thorough research in order to match the advice to your specific situation. The idea is that help is available to help you take action in leveraging credit. You can then teach others, develop programs and courses, that can be lucrative.

Changing Buying Habits

Another important thing to consider in reducing debt is changing your buying habits. Be honest in how you spend. Ask yourself, 'Where is the leak coming from?' for me, I had to change my buying habits by cutting back on fast food and the frequent eating away from home out. If you don't need a particular item, do not buy it! You can also set up your bank accounts so you cannot make withdrawals until a specified time.

The key point is that you have to be conscious of how, and where you're spending your money. There are many ways to apportion your income to minimize your expenditure. For example, 30% savings, 30% expenses, 30% investments, and the remaining 10% you can use for your leisure. This is just one of many ways – change the percentages as is applicable.

Why Do You Want Money Right Now?

Delayed gratification is not easy to do. People living lavish lifestyles are always on display in front of us. Typically, some people try to appear wealthy, acquire many unnecessary material possessions that they are not able to maintain. This is a perfect recipe for heading into debt, and robbing you of quality of life. If your sole reason for wanting money is to 'keep up appearances', I Advise against it. That is hustling backward!

Chapter 7:
Income Streams

While living in the USA and Canada, I discovered a variety of ways to passively make money. Of course I still maintained active and long-term income generation initiatives. Money-making is not about how much you earn; it is about how much you keep. "Gurus" talk about ways to make money all the time, but they fail to break it down well enough for people to understand. In this section, I will be discussing how I generated income in multiple ways.

In society, the norm is to focus on one venture at a time. I do not endorse this principle. What if you can figure out a way to generate multiple streams of income simultaneously? While living in Jamaica, I figured out how to accomplish this; it worked in my favor. Now living in the land of opportunity, I had to learn how to maximize on it! Successful individuals learn how to translate passion into execution. As long as you are passionate, and disciplined, you can develop multiple ways to generate revenue from different niches.

I will reveal some of my secrets to you. You can simply customize them to suit your needs. Always bear in mind that financial freedom is not for the weak, but society's resilient and hardworking people. We are not talking about trading time for money anymore; this is about strategizing and adding value to your existing financial profile.

Famous author Robert Kiyosaki spoke about the four cash flow quadrants, which show how most people live and earn. The *E quadrant*, is basically where people trade time for money. They do the most work, but do not earn most of the profits. The second quadrant *(The S quadrant)* represents those persons who have areas of specialization. These are the small business owners and those who have their professions such as lawyers, doctors, architects, etc. In this quadrant, the business owner spends a minimum of 80 hours per week in the business. They are taxed the heaviest, and if an employee does not show for work, they have to 'pick up the slack'. The third segment is the *B quadrant* which is represents those large business owners with multiple businesses and revenue streams.

To be classified into this quadrant, you will have to work hard and be mentored by someone who is already in this quadrant. This is where the wealthy people of society are. They work 20 hours per week on average, are not taxed much, and they enjoy financial freedom. Likewise, the fourth quadrant represents those persons who we consider to be very wealthy - *super-rich - billionaires*. These people are not only financially free, but their money works for them instead of the other way around. Being a part of the 1% of society is not impossible to achieve, but with the right mindset and mentorship from someone in that group, you can get there. There is a blueprint, so it is your job to follow it. One of the best ways to enter this 'circle' is by joining groups or clubs where your specific niche-oriented mentors are located. Prove yourself by adding value.

The world is changing, and people are discovering new ways of becoming successful, every day. One such way is through real estate. Airbnbs, through technology, have revolutionized the way people generate income from real estate. The internet is the primary means of interacting, whether for business or pleasure. Uber and Lyft, have also disrupted the taxi transportation business. Technology is the way of the future; you can experience freedom by using it to your best advantage!

There are many revenue streams out there that cannot be exhausted in this book, so I will only talk about the streams that I am currently benefiting from: e-commerce, email marketing, affiliate marketing, crypto-currency, real estate, and social media platforms. In addition, some of these income streams complement each other in boosting revenues.

E-commerce

Doing business online is taking over the brick and mortar. The future of business development, and conducting business transactions online is now the norm. Most companies are closing their physical stores and are now moving towards carving out an online presence in order to reduce overhead costs. The Covid-19 pandemic has caused businesses to reduce the need for office space and even staffing. Artificial intelligence and virtual meetings are becoming the norm.

Building online stores, is one way to use the internet to generate income. I used this method to meet the needs of business owners, entrepreneurs, new start-ups, and even skilled professionals who wanted an online presence. There is a need to be recognized and to become easily accessible to customers. I have leveraged the internet in reaching a wider clientele when building and marketing their stores in a functional way.

I was introduced to E-commerce in January 2018 by a friend: Dre. He told me about the potential of building online stores, and using the drop shipping method. Not only could I convert my business from brick and mortar to online, but I could create multiple online stores in different niches, operating at the same time, on the same platform.

My favorite platform is Shopify. After conducting a little personal research, I was able to start the process of building. From my research, I found out that there were many platforms such as Wix, Shopify, WordPress, Vonza, Woo-Commerce, Big Commerce, Square, and Volusion. They all enable the online presence of businesses. Shopify is a straightforward business platform but does not offer much room for creativity. On the other hand, Wix is a bit different. It's a platform that has room for creativity, so I use it to create websites/web pages to fulfill a client's creative product needs.

Shopify is used for my clients who want a straightforward online presence with reduced creativity. My prices range from $200 to $1000 USD, excluding hosting, domain, and other incidental fees. In addition to website creation, I also offer clients marketing opportunities with my Internet marketing arm of the business. In my own businesses, marketing is crucial.

My NiQy hair brand, involves the sale of hair extensions, men's and women's wigs, and fashion accessories. Overtime, the business needed an additional component in order to make the shopping experience easier for customers and business owners. Operating an online business, which involves the selling of physical products, is not easy, so I implemented the drop-shipping method, which helped tremendously! Drop shipping is the method where you serve as the middleman during business-to-business transactions (B2B). It might seem complicated, but it's straightforward, especially on the Shopify platform. There is an app called OBERLO that does the middleman work for you. First, you upload the product from your supplier's website and synchronizes it to your Shopify web store. Then, all you need to do is make a few changes to the text, pictures, prices, before publishing your products!

OBERLO is impressive because all a business would need to do is to monitor the app to ensure that the orders are fulfilled, payments are accepted, and your selected supplier has the product available. Choosing the right supplier is also very important, especially in acquiring the best quality products. One easy approach for quality assurance is to request samples of the product. AliExpress, Dhgate, and Alibaba are some great platforms where you can find suppliers who are willing to do this. If you are more geographically focused, you can contact local suppliers and negotiate with them.

Over time there has been even more creative applications on Shopify that can make operating a business online more manageable. The platform now accommodates shipping, accounting, auto-responding to customers, emails, marketing, and the list goes on. The field of E-commerce is more saturated, as companies are becoming more aware of its many benefits. So for you to be ahead of the competition, and in order to increase your presence and sales, you have to incorporate methods like SEO, email marketing, and running Facebook, YouTube, and other social media ads to reach a wide customer base.

Real Estate

Acquiring Real Estate is one of the best ways to accumulate wealth and earn residual income. To make it big in the traditional real estate market, you have to own a few properties in order to see cash flow coming in. Most people don't have lump sums of money to invest in a few properties, so there has to be an alternative way to establish an entry point into the market. Technological and societal advancements have allowed for easier entry into real estate. Non-traditional means such as Airbnb$_s$ is being endorsed everywhere. This is a new way to turn your property into an asset.

By owning properties, was the route I wanted to take in entering the real estate market. Still, the upfront investment cost would always pose a problem for me. Acquiring properties in Canada is not a walk in the park. It is far easier to achieve properties in the USA. Consider this: typically, a three-bedroom house in the Greater Toronto Area (GTA) valued at $1.5 million CAD, would be equivalent to a property in New York, valuing roughly $500,000 USD. As a young entrepreneur discovering these comparisons, I had to put some real thought into my approach.

I asked real estate agents from Canada, the USA, and the Caribbean, for advice on how, and where to begin. I made one discovery. I could leverage currency exchange. This would enable me to purchase more land and properties at lower rates, if I invest in the Caribbean islands rather than the USA or Canada. Thus, I would receive a greater return on my investment. I figured out why wealthy people invest in the Caribbean islands, and small territories worldwide. Having lived in Jamaica, I recognized that big international companies would build multiple arms of their hotels on the island. I often wondered why? The Sandals resorts brand is very successful in the Caribbean largely because the owners were able to leverage the currency exchange to build more. The AM Resorts Group is also another good example of this.

Consider the following mathematical illustration you can use better understand currency exchange and real estate. Of course, careful considerations and research needs to be conducted before attempting to use this method. It involves taking risks; nonetheless, I will, still give it you.

Example

"Let's Say you have $1 million USD/CAD to invest into the real estate market. In Canada or the USA, that might just be enough for two properties. However, if you invest that 1 million dollars into the real estate market in the Caribbean islands, you would be able to acquire more properties and land. For reference, let's use Jamaica, In Jamaica the current exchange rate is $1USD = $153.99 JMD'; $1CAD = $121. 50 JMD. To illustrate leveraging the currency exchange to enter the real estate market with 1 million; let's use the USD Rate. The 1 million we're investing would covert to $ 1million x 153.990 = a

little over $153 Million JMD. So by leveraging currency exchange, we just turned our 1 million dollars into 153 million Dollars. Wouldn't that be a better amount to start off with? Surely you'll be able to acquire more than two properties with that amount of money. Here's the real deal. Jamaica and the other Caribbean islands are tourist destinations, so the properties you'd be acquiring have the potential to be transformed into weekend getaways, Airbnbs, Hotels, Villas, and the list goes on. With the right marketing approach, you can generate crazy amounts of income, and tailor the prices to the currency you see fit. On top of all that, it is far cheaper to operate and maintain than having such establishments in the USA, UK, Canada, or other first-world countries. The tax breaks would be far more significant, human resources are significantly cheaper, and the cash flow can be endless. "

You can start small, however, ensure that you seek professional advice, conduct thorough research, and contact property management companies to ease the process.

Email Marketing

Email marketing is one of the oldest ways to make money using the internet. However, it's only effective once done using the right strategies and techniques. Typically, using leads from websites or sales funnels, are the primary sources in this revenue stream. You collect emails, and you retarget those same persons by promoting new or existing products in the form of an email. You can also sell your leads to people who want to promote their products. A powerful platform that caters to this service is the name Udimi. This platform is a marketplace for selling and buying leads to generate sales directly or indirectly, through email marketing.

Affiliate Marketing

Affiliate marketing is one of the easiest and fastest ways to generate income online. Affiliate marketing is promoting a product or service created by someone or an entity. You will get a commission when a lead is generated or a sale is made. This type of marketing has been around for many years, and its entry point is cost-effective and straightforward. There are platforms like Clickbank, Digistore24, JVZOOM, and others that primarily create a hub for promoting affiliate products to different audiences. Affiliate marketing has evolved. It's more competitive due to market saturation. To make money on certain products, you have to customize the product you're promoting. You can do this by creating sale funnels or web pages to attract customers.

Another way marketers boost sales are by implementing retargeting plugins on Facebook, Google, and other platforms using pixel integrations. These retarget customers who made, or did not make a purchase. You can also install lead capture plugins that allow retargeting via email or sms. In addition, many businesses create their affiliate system. Platforms like Amazon, Shopify, FashionNova, and others have affiliate programs boosting the earning potential. Not only do you have the chance to buy from them, but you can also earn commissions by referring the products you like to others. This income stream is truly incredible and is a good starting point to earn revenue online, especially if you do not have much money.

Crypto-Currency

Crypto-currency is a digital asset or virtual currency designed to be a payment mechanism that can be exchanged for goods or services. I refer to it as the people's money. As technology evolves, so did the ways to generate income. This will be the new world where digital currency is the new wave, and it soon will replace and devalue the traditional dollar. Crypto-currency is classified as people's money mainly because a government does not control it (at this time). Instead, it is controlled by the people, and the people determine its value.

This new currency has a lot of skepticism surrounding it. That is because we genuinely do not know what digital assets and blockchain technology represent. However, most of the crypto-currency assets are decentralized. Decentralization is where we as a people have more power and control collectively. Digital currencies give a type of monetary freedom. We have a taste of it for now, at least, while government bodies are working on ways to control the system (forgive me for that negative projection but it's the truth). Many financial institutions were, and still are against digital currencies being used, however, we can see that this is changing as time progresses.

Bitcoin has grown in popularity and is very valuable. It has the most significant market capital in the industry, and is often referred to as digital gold. Ethereum, Cardona, Solana, and Doge are also top-rated coins among hundreds of other digital currencies that are out there. " The point is, this type of currency isn't globalized yet, and so many are ignorant of it. Now is the time to invest, so you can capitalize on increased gains; the market is growing. Knowing how to invest is readily available in all types and forms. If you want gold, you have to dig for it.

Crypto investing is one of the best ways to earn money, not because its money-generating possibilities are similar to stocks options, futures, and forex trading. The real advantage is that the price is meager, so increasing your gains tenfold is even more possible. The cryptocurrency market is very volatile, some say, but the stock market is as well! Here is how I've profited from Crypto investing:

Around March 2020, when all the world economies crashed due to the covid19 Pandemic, the cryptocurrency market was also hit. That was when I decided to enter the market. It was very risky, but I took action and hopped in because the prices were very low. There is a saying that you buy low and sell high, and that is what I did. Bitcoin had a value of $20,000 and dropped to $5,000 due to the market crash. Many people would say that it would be a crazy time to do such a thing. However, I followed my gut feeling. I entered with $500; although the market was going down rapidly, I was confident in my decision because I knew that the market would rise again eventually.

A few months later, the market went up back, and the bitcoin price went from $5000 to $61,000. My investment of $500 increased more than ten times, turning a massive profit for me! As the economy stabilized, the Ethereum coin was my next target because it had the second-largest market cap. I followed the same strategy but raised the investment to $1,500 CAD. The price for Ethereum was $1,200 per share at the time of purchase. After which, the coin increased up to $5,200 per share! Profits yet again.

Lesson: We have to develop self-confidence and believe in ourselves. I could have doubted myself but chose to go all in and trust the process. This scenario illustrates the money-generating power of crypto-currency, but that isn't all. The true power of digital assets and crypto-currencies has not been fully tapped into yet. There are a thousand fold projections for some of the upcoming coins. because the market is so unsaturated. Conduct your market research and start looking into crypto-currency investments to experience these possibilities for yourself.

Social Media Platforms

The common ways of generating income have changed and evolved into something unexpected over the last decade. Social media is now one of the most significant ways to generate income; mainly by monetizing content and running ads against them. The most popular platforms are Facebook, YouTube, TikTok, Snapchat, Twitter, Linked In, and Instagram. Money is generated from these platforms by running ads. Each platform has developed its cutting-edge monetization features that the new generation and even more mature people are capitalizing on. Influencer marketing is on the rise. The more followers you have, the more reach you will have generating massive income.

YouTube is a social media platform that allows you to post videos that live perpetually. To maximize the earning potential of this platform, most people create their web channels. They post videos, and the more engagement the video gets through likes, comments, subscribers, the further the videos are pushed up the rankings. Commissions are paid out to those who have the most popular videos. The more engagement you have, the more you are paid.

YouTube pays you based on the ads attached to your videos. That being said, the more engaging videos are, the higher the possibility of a person clicking on an ad. You have to get at least a thousand subscribers to your channel and at least four thousand watch hours in one year to qualify for the monetization program (at this time). Some people have become great at running affiliate links against their videos to generate revenue as well. YouTube is still to this day a gold mine for income streams.

Facebook is another platform that incorporates the ads-based income-generating feature as well. People pay to advertise goods and services, and they also allow social interaction or networking among peers. Facebook users use web posts, fan pages, groups, videos, pictures, and status updates to generate revenue. Instagram (IG) is a platform owned by Facebook, which is typically used by a younger audience. Becoming an influencer on IG generates a lot of money.

LinkedIn is another opportunity channel. LinkedIn primarily functions as a business-oriented, job recruiting, and job-seeking interaction hub where people and entities communicate and share ideas. The platform's money generating process is similar to Facebook's by the use of ads. TikTok is also a rising giant and shares similarities to IG. People post video content, and run ads. Based on engagement, they receive revenue from the platform.

There are multiple ways to generate income from social media platforms, and these are just a few. As time goes by, new methods will come, and new revenue-generating tactics will become available. What will you do when the opportunity arises? Will you miss it?

Final Thoughts

Life is like a chess game. You will lose or win; GAMBIT's will have to be made, but the most important thing is what you do with the opportunity at hand! The journey for everyone will not be the same. However, no matter how early or late, the choices we make will determine the quality of life we have in the end. Often, we blame people, the environment, and even God for the misfortunes we have. We forget about the prime suspects: ourselves. Taking responsibility for the actions and decisions we make will bring us to a higher level of thinking and maturity, which is the key to unlocking your inner potential.

Being wealthy or successful isn't by chance. Our thinking pattern is what determines who becomes rich or poor. The mindset we possess will determine the result of any action we take to solve any issue. Positive thinking will result in positive results, while negative thinking with give you undesirable results. God gives all of us blessings, opportunities, and talents. How we identify and use these incredible gifts will determine our success level. Selflessly adding value to our fellow man is the real deal. That is what it means to have BIG PROFITS. The more you give, the more you receive!

I hope you enjoyed, or learned something from this book. Please share it with others so they too can be enlightened!

Made in the USA
Middletown, DE
08 June 2024